The
Wonderful
O

by
James Thurber

Illustrated by Marc Simont

Simon and Schuster
New York

For Ted Gardiner
and his Julias and Patricias,
with love and other good O words.

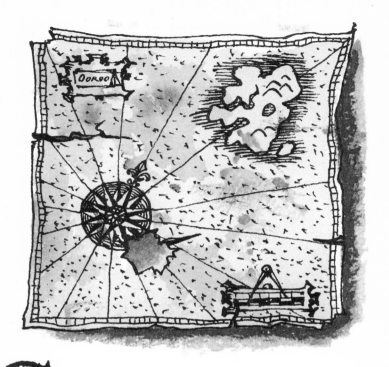

Somewhere a ponderous tower clock slowly dropped a dozen strokes into the gloom. Storm clouds rode low along the horizon, and no moon shone. Only a melancholy chorus of frogs broke the soundlessness. Then a strange figure appeared out of the nocturnal somnolence, as unexpectedly as the blare of a bugle in a lullaby. He entered the tavern near the sea, and a blade of light flashed into the blackness and disappeared when the old oaken door closed once more.

The newcomer was a seafaring man, and the sight of him turned the taverners silent. There was a green parrot on the man's shoulder, and a tarred pigtail hung down his back. He carried no crutch, for he had two legs, and he rolled like a goose when he walked. His voice when he spoke was as deep as a gong in a tomb.

"Call me Littlejack!" he roared, and the taverners called him Littlejack.

A lean, silent man at a shadowy table in a corner, wearing a black cape and black gloves, beckoned to the newcomer, who sat down across from him. "You look like a man with a map," whispered the man in black.

"I am a man with a map," boomed Littlejack. "It is a map of a far and lonely island, rich with jewels, sapphires, emeralds, and rubies. I seek a man with a ship."

"I am a man with a ship," said the man in black.

"And a crew to man her?"

"And a crew to man her."

"Are you a man with a name?" asked Littlejack.

"I am a man named Black," said the man named Black. They shook hands, one heavy and bare, the other thin and gloved, and reached a bargain at one o'clock: "Two-thirds of the booty for me and you, the other third will go to the crew."

Black smiled, and when he smiled he showed his lower teeth. "Now let me see the map," he said. And he took the map and studied it. "There are no crosses here," said Black, "or marks. There should be crosses here and marks, indicating where the jewels lie hidden."

"There is another map with marks and crosses, but what became of it and where it is, no man can say," said Littlejack.

"We'll find the map, or if we don't, we'll find the jewels without it," Black declared. He gazed at Littlejack as if the sailor were a jigsaw puzzle that had too many parts, or not enough. "You have the mien and manner of a man out of the past. Where do you come from?"

The sailor grinned. "Not, matey, from the regions which are wholly land. I'll take the map."

"It's safe with me," said Black.

"It's safer if we cut the thing in two," said Little-jack. And with his cutlass he cut the map in two. And Black took half of it and Littlejack the other half.

They went aboard the ship at two o'clock. "I can't

make out her name," said Littlejack. "How is she called?"

"The *Aeiu*," said Black.

"A weird, uncanny name," the sailor said. "It sounds a little like a night bird screaming."

"It's all the vowels except the O," Black said. "I've had a hatred of that letter ever since the night my mother became wedged in a porthole. We couldn't pull her in and so we had to push her out." He shuddered and his eyes turned hard. "What is the name of this island?" he asked, shaking off the thought of O.

"Ooroo," said Littlejack, and once more the other shuddered.

"I hate the name," he said at last. "It sounds like the eyes of a couple of ghosts leaning against an R. I speak O-words myself, so I can spit them out." Something screamed. "A night bird," whispered Black. "The sailors say it's my mother. Let's go below. I've got a cabin full of rum."

4

When the dawn came up the *Aeiu,* whose sails were black as raven wings, could no longer be seen from shore, even by the sharpest eye and strongest glass. The weather was fair and the voyage was long. Then early one morning the ship came into the only port of the far and lonely island, and Black and Littlejack went ashore, the former softly, and the latter swaggering, followed by their surly and sinewy crew.

"We have come for your jewels," Black told a spokesman of the quiet people, "with cutlasses and pistols."

"With axes and spades and cudgels," said Littlejack.

"We have no jewels," said the spokesman, "except

the blue of the water, and the pink of our maidens'
cheeks and lips, and the green of our fields."

"We have come for your jewels," repeated Black.

"We have only moonstones and opals, and other
ordinary stones," the spokesman said.

"Ordinary stones, ordinary stones!" squawked the
green parrot.

"There is a map," said Black, "a secret map, with
marks and crosses, indicating where the jewels lie
hidden."

"I know of no such map," the spokesman said.

Black grinned and showed his lower teeth again.
"Take the town apart," he cried, and the crew began
taking the town apart, with axes and spades and cud-

gels, smashing the locks off doors, prying the lids from boxes, breaking into closets and cupboards, but all they found was moonstones and opals and other ordinary stones, lockets and lovenotes, options, contracts, mortgages, records, reports, and other documents, but neither precious stones nor any map.

"Dig in the woods," commanded Black.

"Dig in the meadows," ordered Littlejack. And the crew dug in the woods and in the meadows, but all they found was owls in oaks, moss and moles, toads and toadstools, roots and rocks.

"Drain the brooks," snarled Black.

"Drain the pools," roared Littlejack. And the crew drained the brooks and the pools, but all they found was trout and tortoises, frogs and worms, and an owl that had drowned in a pool.

"Owls in oaks, owls in pools!" squawked the parrot.

The crew then turned to towers and fountains with their axes and cudgels, but all they got for their sweat and pains was the stones that towers are built of, and the sparkle of fountain water.

That night Black and Littlejack sat at a table in a tavern, drinking rum from tankards. "There must be sapphires," whispered Black.

"And emeralds and rubies," grumbled Littlejack.

"Opals and moonstones," squawked the parrot. "Lovenotes, lockets, options. Owls in oaks, moss and moles, and mortgages."

"Stop his squawking," Black exclaimed, "or else I'll squck his thrug till all he can whupple is geep."

"All he can whupple is geep, all he can whupple is geep," squawked the parrot.

"Still, I'm glad he named the things we found," said Black, after a moment. "Everything we find has an O in its name, and everywhere we look has an O in its name, and everything we open—closets, cupboards, woods, meadows."

"Floors and roofs," added Littlejack, "and brooks and pools."

Black stared into his tankard, while the tavern clock ticked sixty times. "I hate things with an O in their names," cried Black. "That goes for clocks and parrots." He threw his tankard at the clock and broke it open, but there was nothing inside but works, no rubies, no emeralds, and no sapphires, and no map.

8

"The parrot's name's Magraw," said Littlejack. "There ain't no O in that."

"Squck his thrug," squawked the parrot. "Squck his thrug."

"And there ain't no O in that," said Littlejack.

Black stood up and smote the table with his fist. "I'll get rid of O, in upper case and lower," cried the man in black. "I'll issue an edict. All words in books or signs with an O in them shall have the O erased or painted out. We'll print new books and paint new signs without an O in them."

And so the locksmith became a lcksmith, and the bootmaker a btmaker, and people whispered like conspirators when they said the names. *Love's Labour's Lost* and *Mother Goose* flattened out like a pricked balloon. Books were bks and Robinhood was Rbinhd. Little Goody Two Shoes lost her O's and so did Goldilocks, and the former became a whisper, and the latter sounded like a key jiggled in a lck. It was impossible to read "cockadoodledoo" aloud, and parents gave up reading to their children, and some gave up reading altogether, and the search for the precious jewels went on.

The afternoon after the night at the tavern, while O's were being taken out of books and out of signs, so that the cw jumped over the mn, and the dish ran

9

away with the spn, and the clockshop became a clckshp, the toymaker a tymaker, Black issued new searching orders. "Look in violins and cellos," he commanded.

"Look in trombones, horns, and oboes," thundered Littlejack. And the crew looked in violins and cellos, trombones, horns, and oboes, piccolos and banjos, finding nothing, for nothing came out of them except music.

That night in the tavern, after his thirteenth pint of rum, Black began to sing a ditty in a voice that had the timbre of a buzzard's:

> *"I won't go down the horrible street*
> *To see the horrible people.*
> *I'll gladly climb the terrible stair*
> *That leads to the terrible steeple*
> *And the terrible bats, and the terrible*
> *   rats,*
> *And the cats in the terrible steeple.*
> *But I won't go down the horrible street*
> *To see the horrible people."*

As he sang, the taverners stared at him and then they left their drinks unfinished, paid for them, and slunk away into the night.

"Methinks the people have a loathing for your voice and for your song," said Littlejack.

"I'll take away from them," said Black, "everything that plays and has an O."

And so the following morning the crew went from house to house, seizing violins and cellos, trombones, horns and oboes, pianos, harpsichords, and clavichords, accordions and melodeons, bassoons and saxophones, and all the other instruments with O's, up to and including the woodwinds. A man and his

wife who loved to play duets on mandolin and glockenspiel drifted apart. Children, forbidden the use
of combs, could no longer play tunes on combs with
tissue paper. The crew spent the afternoon breaking
up an old calliope they had found rusting in a field,
and taking apart a carillon.

"All they have is fifes and drums and cymbals,"
gloated Black.

"And zithers and guitars," said Littlejack. "And
dulcimers and spinets, and bugles, harps and trum-
pets."

"Much good they'll get from these," said Black,
"or any others. I haven't finished with the O's in
music, in harmony and melody, that is, and compo-

sitions. They'll have no score, and what is more,
no orchestra, or podium, or baton, and no conductor.
They can't play symphonies, or rhapsodies, sonatas
or concerti. I'll take away their oratorios and choirs
and choruses, and all their soloists, their baritones and
tenors and sopranos, their altos and contraltos and
accompanists. All they'll have is the funeral march,
the chant and anthem, and the dirge, and certain
snatches."

"They'll still have serenades," said Littlejack.

Black made an evil and impatient gesture. "You
can't serenade a lady on a balcony," he said, "if there
isn't any balcony. Let them hum their hymns and
lisp their litanies." Black's eyes began to glow as he

named O-names that would have to go: "Scherzo, largo, and crescendo, allegro and diminuendo. Let the lyric writers have their Night in June. Much good it'll do 'em without the moon." He crushed an imaginary moon in his hand. "At least the people cannot dance the polka, or the schottische, or gavotte. I wish they mourned their loss, here on R, but they do not."

"R?" asked Littlejack.

"I've taken the O's out of Ooroo," Black explained. "Isles with O's in their names are few, and invariably unlucky, such as the Isle of Lyonesse, which sank into the sea. I've made a list of isles still standing, none of which has a trace of O. It must mean something." He pulled a parchment from his pocket and read the names of O-less isles aloud: "Iceland, Greenland, England, Wales, and Ireland; Jersey, Guernsey, Man and Wight; Capri, Crete, and Cyprus; Elba, Malta, and St. Helena; Madagascar, Zanzibar, Sardinia—"

"St. Helena and Elba," said Littlejack, "were not too lucky for Napoleon."

"Napoleon Bonaparte," said Black, "was born on Corsica. His bad luck started there." And then he resumed the reading of his list: "Bali and the Baleares, the Philippines and Celebes, the Fijis and the Hebrides, Cuba and Bermuda, the East Indies and

14

West Indies, the Lesser and the Greater Antilles, Martinique and Trinidad, Easter and Jamaica, the Virgins and Canaries, Sicily and Haiti and Hawaii. And add a T to Haiti for Tahiti." His voice gave out before the list was finished.

Littlejack closed one eye and said, "You left out one. A friend of mine named Gunn lived there, if you could call it living."

"Its name," breathed Black, "is Treasure."

That night the people of the town and those who lived in the country met secretly in the woods. They had been called together by a poet named Andreus, who read aloud, or tried to read, a poem he had just had printed at the printer's. It was called "The Mn Belngs T Lvers," but the poetry had died in it with the death of its O's. "Soon Black and Littlejack," said Andreus, "will no longer let us live in houses, for houses have an O."

"Or cottages," said the blacksmith, "for cottage has an O, and so does bungalow."

"We'll have to live in huts," the baker said, "or shacks, or sheds, or shanties, or in cabins."

"Cabins without logs," said Andreus. "We shall have mantels but no clocks, shelves without crocks, keys without locks, walls without doors, rugs without floors, frames without windows, chimneys with no roofs to put them on, knives without a fork or spoon, beds without pillows. There will be no wood for our fires, no oil for our lamps, and no hobs for our kettles."

"They will take my dough," moaned the baker.

"They will take my gold," moaned the goldsmith.

"And my forge," sighed the blacksmith.

"And my cloth," wept the tailor.

"And my chocolate," muttered the candymaker.

At this a man named Hyde arose and spoke. "Chocolate is bad for the stomach," he said. "We shall still have wintergreen and peppermint. Hail to Black and Littlejack, who will liberate us all from licorice and horehound!"

"Hyde is a lawyer," Andreus pointed out, "and he will still have his fees and fines."

"And his quills and ink," said the baker.

"And his paper and parchment," said the goldsmith.

"And his chair and desk," said the blacksmith.

"And his signs and seals," said the tailor.

"And his briefs and liens," said the candymaker.

But the lawyer waved them all aside. "We shall all have an equal lack of opportunity," he said smoothly. "We shall all have the same amount of nothing. There must be precious jewels, or Black and Littlejack would not have come so far to search for them. I suggest we look in nooks and corners and in pigeonholes ourselves." Some of the men agreed with Hyde, but most of them took the poet's side.

"We must think of a way to save our homes," the poet said. And they sat on the ground until the moon went down, trying to think of a way. And even as they thought, Black and Littlejack and their men were busily breaking open dolls, and yellow croquet balls, and coconuts, but all they found was what is always found in dolls, and yellow croquet balls, and coconuts.

The next morning Andreus was walking with his poodle in a street whose cobblestones had been torn up in the search for jewels when he encountered Black and Littlejack.

"You are *both* pets now," sneered Littlejack, "for the

O has gone out of poet, and out of trochee and strophe and spondee, and ode and sonnet and rondeau."

The poodle growled.

"I hate poodles," snarled Black, "for poodles have a double O."

"My pet is French," said Andreus. "He is not only a *chien*, which is French for dog, but a *caniche*, which is French for poodle."

"*Chien caniche*," squawked the parrot. "*Chien caniche*."

"Then I will get rid of the other domestic creatures with an O," cried Black, and he issued an edict to this effect.

There was great consternation on the island now, for people could have pigs, but no hogs or pork or bacon; sheep, but no mutton or wool; calves, but no cows. Geese were safe as long as one of them did not stray from the rest and become a goose, and if one of a family of mice wandered from the nest, he became a mouse and lost his impunity. Children lost their ponies, and farmers their colts and horses and goats and their donkeys and their oxen.

Test cases were constantly brought to court—or curt, as it was called. "Somebody will have to clarify the law for everybody, or nobody will know where anybody stands," the people said. So Black appointed

19

Hyde lawyer, judge, and chief clarifier. "The more chaotic the clarification," said Black, "the better. Remember how I hate that letter."

This was right up Hyde's dark and devious alley. "Chaotic is now chatic," he said, "a cross between chaos and static." He decided that farmers could keep their cows if they kept them in herds, for cows in herds are kine or cattle. And so the people had milk and cheese and butter. He decided in favor

of hens and eggs, if hens were segregated. "Keep them out of flocks," he said, "for flocks are not only flocks, but also poultry."

"We have no corn or potatoes, or cauliflower or tomatoes," a housewife said one day.

"In a vegetable garden," said Hyde, "the things that grow are ninety-five per cent without an O. I could name you twenty such," he added cockily, "and then you'd scream in unison for broccoli. Almost all the fruits are yours to eat, from the apple to the tangerine, with a good two dozen in between. I'll stick to those that start with P to show you what I mean: the pear, the peach, the plum, the prune, the plantain and pineapple, the pawpaw and papaya. But you will yearn for things you never ate, and cannot tolerate—I know you women—the pomegranate, for one, and the dull persimmon. No grapefruit, by the way. I hate its bitter juice. I have banned it, under its French name, *pamplemousse*."

Another wife took the stand one day to complain of the things she hadn't. "Cloves and cinnamon," she said, "and marjoram and saffron."

"You still have dill," said Hyde, "and thyme and sage and basil, vinegar, vanilla, and sarsaparilla, salt and pepper and paprika, ginger and the spices. You can't have coffee, but there is tea; to sweeten it, there's sugar."

A seamstress raised her hand to ask about the O's in textiles, fabrics, and in clothes. "You're denied a few," admitted Hyde. "Corduroy and bombazine, organdy and tricotine, calico and crinoline. But you have silk and satin, velvet, lace and linen, tulle and twill and tweed, damask and denim, madras and muslin, felt and chintz and baize and leather, and twenty more for cool and warm and winter weather."

Now the boatswain of the crew was a man named Stragg and the cockswain was a man named Strugg, and the former was allergic to roses, and the latter was allergic to phlox. So Black decided that even the flowers with an O in their names were against him, and he ordered his crew to get rid of roses and phlox in the gardens of the island, and oleanders and moonflowers and morning-glories, and cosmos and coxcomb and columbine, and all the rest with O's.

"But my livelihood is violets and hollyhocks and marigold," a gardener complained.

"Lilies are nice for livelihood," said Hyde, "and more alliterative. There are also lilacs and the like. I crossbreed certain things myself, with more success than failure. Forget-me-nots, when crossed with madwort, lose their O's. I get a hybrid which I call regret-me-evers. Love-in-a-mist, when crossed with bleeding hearts, results in sweethearts' quarrels."

"It's blasphemy or heresy," the women cried, "or something!"

"You haven't heard the half of it," said Hyde. "Black-eyed susans, crossed with ragged sailors, give me ragged susans. Jack-in-the-pulpit, crossed with devil's paintbrush, should give me devil-in-the-pulpit. And think of the fine satanic chimes that will emerge from hellebore crossed with Canterbury bells." At this the women rose in anger and dismay and left the curt without a curtsy.

"Why not get rid of all the flowers?" demanded Black one day. "After all, there is an O in flowers."

"I thought of that," said Hyde, "but we must spare collective nouns, like food, and goods, and crops, and tools, and, I should think, the lesser schools. I have taken the carpenter's gouge and boards. It still leaves him much too much, but that's the way it goes, with and without O's. He has his saw and ax and hatchet, his hammer and his chisel, his brace and bit, and plane and level, also nails and tacks and brads and screws and staples. But all he can build is bric-abrac and knickknack, gewgaw, kickshaw, and gimcrack. No coop or goathouse, no stoop or boathouse."

"I would that I could banish body; then I'd get rid of everybody." Black's eyes gleamed like rubies. "No more anatomy, and no morphology, physiognomy, or physiology, or people, or even persons. I think about it often in the night. Body is blood and bones and other O's, organs, torso, abdomen, and toes."

Hyde curled his upper lip. "I'll build you a better man," he said, "of firmer flesh and all complete, from hairy head to metatarsal feet, using A's and I's and U's and E's, with muscular arms and flexible knees; eyes and ears and lids and lips, neck and chest and breast and hips; liver, heart and lungs and chin, nerves and ligaments and skin; kidneys, pancreas and flanks, ankles, calves and shins and shanks; legs and lashes, ribs and spleen—" Black had turned a little green, and then Hyde held up both his hands. "Brains and veins and cells and glands—"

"Silence!" thundered Black. "I wish that more things had an O."

Hyde sighed. "There is no O in everything," he said. "We can't change that."

"I will not take their vocal cords, or tongues, or throats," said Black, "but I shall make these jewelhiders speak without the use of O in any word they say."

And so language and the spoken word diminished and declined as the people were forced to speak without the use of O in any word. No longer could the people say Heigh-Ho, Yoohoo, or Yo ho ho, or even plain Hello. The theater in the town was closed, for Shakespeare's lines without an O sound flat and muffled. No one could play *Othello* when *Othello* turned to *Thell*, and Desdemona was strangled at the start. Some sentences became so strange they sounded like a foreign tongue. "Dius gre gling minus gress" meant "Odious ogre ogling ominous ogress," but only scholars knew it. Spoken words became a hissing and a mumble, or a murmur and a hum. A man named Otto Ott, when asked his name, could only stutter. Ophelia Oliver repeated hers, and vanished from the haunts of men.

"We can't tell shot from shoot, or hot from hoot," the blacksmith said, in secret meeting with his fellows.

"We can't tell rot from root, or owed from wed," the baker said.

"It's even worse than that," said Andreus, "for oft becomes the same as foot, and odd the same as dodo. Something must be done at once, or we shall never know what we are saying." And he was right. Some people said that moles were mulls, while others

called them emmels. The author of a book called
Flamingo Stories read *Flaming Stries* aloud to his
wife, and gave up writing.

"I still hear laughter," Black complained to Hyde
one day. "After all I've done to them I still hear
laughter."

"There is no O in laughter," Hyde reminded him,
"or in smile, or grin, or giggle. There is, of course,
an O in chortle, but none in chuckle or in snicker."

"Don't play games with me!" snarled Black.

"Games," he repeated, chewing the word as if it were candy. "Take their Yo-yos and diavolos and dominoes; throw their quoits and shuttlecocks away, and everything pertaining to croquet; shuffleboard and crochinole must go, Post Office, Pillow, and ticktacktoe. Ping-pong—"

Hyde raised his hand in quick dissent. "Table tennis," he said, "is played with O-less paddles, balls and net, upon an O-less table."

Black went on naming the names of what were now illegal games. "Let them play tiddlywinks," said Black, "and mumblety-peg."

Hyde recruited a dozen men, and soon a dozen others were helping them to keep the people from playing certain games at night in cellars—leapfrog, hopscotch, and Pussy Wants a Corner.

"We live in peril and in danger," Andreus told the people, "and in a little time may have left few things that we can say. Already there is little we can play. I have a piece that I shall read. It indicates the quandary we're in." And then he read it:

"They are swing chas. What is slid? What is left

28

that's slace? We are begne and webegne. Life is bring and brish. Even schling is flish. Animals in the z are less lacnic than we. Vices are filled with paths and scial intercurse is baths. Let us gird up ur lins like lins and rt the hrrr and ust the afs."

"What nannibickering is this?" cried the blacksmith. "What is this gibberish?"

"English," said Andreus, "without its O's." And he read the piece again with all its O's and double O's. Many had figured webegne was woebegone, but none could tell that begne was obegone.

"How shall we dispel this nightmare of flishness?" demanded the baker, who could not say f for of.

"The answer must lie," said Andreus, "in what has been written. I suggest that we all read what we have left in libraries, searching the secret, hunting the scheme and spell that may bring an end to Black and Littlejack."

It was dark in the woods that night, and Andreus and his followers did not realize that Hyde listened

to their plans, concealed behind a tree. He had been barred from bar and meetings by his colleagues and his countrymen. The next morning the outlawed lawyer went to Black and told what he had heard.

"Destroy all books that might be helpful," commanded Black, "especially those dealing with studies and sciences that have O's in their names: geography, biography, biology, psychology, philosophy, philology, astronomy, agronomy, gastronomy; trigonometry, geometry, optometry, and all the other ologies and onomies and ometries."

The crew set about their new task with a will, and before they were through they had torn down colleges and destroyed many a book and tome and volume, and globe and blackboard and pointer, and banished professors, assistant professors, scholars, tutors, and instructors. There was no one left to translate English into English. Babies often made as much sense as their fathers.

There walked in beauty on the island a maiden named Andrea. In her father's library one night, searching for the secret and the spell that might confound the vandals and in the end get rid of them, she found an ancient book of magic. The next night Andrea brought the book to the secret meeting in the woods. Andreus was fearful, for women had not been permitted to take part in the meetings. The poet was afraid that women might be banished from the island because of the O in women and in woman.

"They would banish mothers, too," said Andreus, forgetting to speak in words without an O.

"A maiden is safe as a maiden," Andrea pointed out, "and as a lass, or girl, or damsel, and as virgin and as spinster."

"And as a darling and a dear," said Andreus. "But still you are a woman."

"I could become a bride and wife," said Andrea. "Bride and wife are more than woman."

"Then you would be a matron," said Andreus, "without the hope of tot or toddler, boy or moppet."

"Enough of this puppybabble and pussyfret," the wheelwright whined. "I have no spokes for my wheels, and wheels without spokes are like words without O's."

"I have no tallow for my candles," complained the candlemaker, "and candles without tallow are not candles."

"Be not afraid to speak with O's," said Andrea at last. "We cannot live or speak without hope, and hope without its O is nothing, and even nothing is less than nothing when it is nthing. Hope contains the longest O of all. We mustn't lose it." Thereupon she gave Andreus the book she had found in her father's library.

"It is called *The Enchanted Castle*," said Andreus.

"I know the book," quavered an old man with a white beard, "and I can tell you what it says, and spare you the time and trouble of reading a book aloud that has no O's in any word."

"Then tell us what it says," cried Andreus, "for it is full of footnotes which are now called ftntes."

The old man cleared his throat and spoke. "Listen, my children, and you shall hear of a magical castle which will appear one month from tonight in this very year." And he told the tale of the enchanted castle, while the others listened in silence. "There was a king upon this island once, a thousand years ago, but he was driven from his castle by such a crew of bashlocks and shatterclocks as plagues us now. They took the castle apart and down, stone by stone, searching for precious jewels or a map which were not there, or, if they were, could not be found. The king was banished from the island, but as he left he put a wondrous spell upon the ground where once the castle stood." The old man stopped to scratch his head.

"How runs this spell?" demanded Andreus.

"Perhaps the maiden here remembers. My mem-

ory is no longer what it was," the old man said.

"Every hundred years the castle shall appear again," Andrea said, "in semblance and in seeming, an enchanted castle, such as children see when they are dreaming."

"And who may enter there?" asked Andreus. "And why and wherefore?"

Andrea raised her hands and let them fall. "The last page of the book is lost," she said.

"The last page of the book contained a map," the old man murmured. "My memory isn't what it was, but I remember that." He stood awhile in silence, then went on. "Whoever finds the map will find a jewel in everything he opens. My memory isn't what it was, but I remember that."

"Where is this map?" asked Andreus. "Can you remember that?"

The old man thought and thought before he spoke.

"It's on a wall, I seem to recall, an old wall in the castle. Whoever finds it will find a certain jewel without which men are lost."

"Then we shall be first upon the scene when the castle reappears," cried Andreus.

The old man shook his head in gloom. "Only evil men may enter there," he said. "So runs the royal spell. I know not why, and if I ever knew, I have forgotten."

"Then we are lost," said Andreus.

"We can't be lost when lost has lost its O," the old man said. "Or can we?"

The others turned away lest they reveal the look of doom upon their faces. The old man spoke again. "I seem to hear a strange new bell, an old familiar bell, a bell I never heard before, a bell that I remember."

The others turned to him and stared. And in the gloom Andrea whispered, "A bell of triumph, or a knell?"

"Time," the old man sighed, "will tell."

The vandals spent the next day breaking into cupolas and cracking open cornices and cornerstones, smashing gargoyles into bits, and razing marble columns, Ionic, Doric, Gothic, and Corinthian, and everything baroque or rococo. In one cool, cloistered corridor Black himself smashed with an ax marble busts of Homer and Horace and Plato, Ovid and Omar and Cato, Diogenes and Damocles, Socrates and Hippocrates, and Demosthenes and Aristophanes. Not a single sparkle sparkled in the rubble.

"Why don't we open tombs?" Littlejack inquired one day. "Jewels are often hid in tombs."

"Tombs are in cemeteries," Black replied. "I have come to hold a great respect for words that have no O. That is why we shall invade no shrine, or church, or chapel."

"Perhaps you have a certain dread of ghosts and ghouls," said Littlejack. "They howl in O, you know, and so do goblins and hobgoblins. But spooks and phantoms have an O we cannot touch."

"I hate all O's I cannot touch," Black muttered with a shudder.

"The alphabet has taken over," Littlejack complained. "What was the letter of the law is now the law of the letter."

"Nonetheless, we search no place without an O," said Black. "That is why I've left untouched the jungle and the desert and the swamp, the wilderness and wasteland. Besides, they're full of animals with A and E and I and U in all their names: the camel and the elephant, the aardvark and the platypus, the yak, the zebra, and the gnu, the tiger and the jaguar, the panther and the puma and the lynx. I have a certain liking now for creatures of this kind."

"*I* have a certain fear of animals with O," said Littlejack, "I know not why."

"I happen to know there are no animals with O," said Black. "I'll tell you why. There is a man named Filch among the crew."

"A sticky-fingered lad," said Littlejack.

"Whose sticky fingers found an ancient document somewhere among the ruins we have made," said Black.

"How goes this document?" asked Littlejack.

Black showed his lower teeth. "It tells of how a king in olden times, whose niece was bitten by a crocodile, banished all the larger animals with O

39

from desert, swamp, and jungle—the crocodile, the lion, and the boar, the python and the cobra and the boa, the gorilla and the gibbon and the wolf. Orangutans and baboons disappeared. The porcupine, the mongoose, and the sloth, the dingo and the leopard and the potto were driven from their tree, or cave, or grotto."

"The rhinoceros and the hippopotamus?" asked Littlejack.

"Gone with the otter and the kangaroo," said Black. "There are no creatures left with O here on this island, except a few so small they cannot plague us." And once again that night he said, seated in the tavern, "There are no animals with O to plague us."

A barmaid heard his words, and when her work was done she joined the others at their secret meet-

ing in the woods and told them all what Black had
said. And at this moment Hyde appeared among
them, as if from nowhere. "Your furred and finned
and feathered friends with O are either gone, or
quite extinct, or never were!" he cried. "The dino-
saur and the brontosaurus, the mammoth and the
behemoth, old ichthyosaurus and the pterodactyl,
the dodo and the mastodon." He turned to Andreus
and said sarcastically, "The only other animals with
O are mythical. Why don't you call on them for help?"

"What animals are these that never were?" the old
man asked. "My memory isn't what it was, you know.
I find it very hard to think of things that haven't
been."

"The unicorn, the dragon, and the Minotaur,"
said Hyde, "demons out of legend and of lore—the
griffon and the cockatrice, the Phoenix and the Gor-
gon and the roc, the ogo-pogo and the monster in the
Loch. And if these ten don't make a quorum, why,

call upon the cockalorum." The moon had gone behind a cloud and the people felt cold and fearful, as if they had lost, somehow, their only allies. "The animals with A and E and I and U are on the side of Black and Littlejack," said Hyde, "and that is all there are. Unless, of course, you count the creatures with an O one finds in fairy tales and fantasies—the tove, the mome rath, and the borogove, the whiffen-poof and wogglebug and Dong, the Pod, the Todal, and the gorm."

"I never heard of gorms," the old man said, "or Todals."

"That's because they never were," said Hyde, "except in books, where they are not your friend but foe, since each of them has lost its O." He left the group and disappeared among the trees, and they could hear his mocking laughter as he went.

Andrea had fallen silent, but now she spoke as if reciting something: "There are four words with O. You musn't lose them. Find out what they are and learn to use them."

"Hope is one," said Andreus.

"And love," said Andrea.

"And valor, I should think," the old man said. And then they tried to find the fourth, naming courage, thought, and reason, devotion, work, and worship.

"None of these is right," said Andrea. "I'll know it when I hear it." And so, until the setting of the moon, they tried out words with O—imagination and religion, dedication and decision, honor, progeny, and vision. "None of these is the word," said Andrea. "I'll know it when I hear it."

"I hope," the old man said, "we think of it in time. Perhaps the word is wisdom."

"An austere word," Andrea said, "but surely not the greatest." And they spent the rest of the night searching for the greatest, trying youth and joy and jubilation, victory and exaltation, languor, comfort, relaxation, money, fortune, non-taxation, motherhood and domesticity, and many anotherhood and icity. But Andrea shook her lovely head at every word the people said, rejecting soul and contemplation, dismissing courtship and elation, and many anothership and ation.

"I miss the O," the old man said, "in faith and truth and beauty. The O belongs, alas, to lost and gone, forsaken and forgotten." The others felt forlorn at this, but still the search continued, in all the hopes and dreams of men, from action to euphoria. The

43

old man stroked his beard and said, "*Sic transit verbi gloria.*"

There still were those who spoke with O's, and one of these was a boatwright, a man of force and gusto. "You are still my spouse and not my spuse," he told his fearful wife, "and this is my house and not my huse, and I make boats, not bats, and I wear coats, not cats. What," he asked his youngest son, "did you learn today in school?"

"It's schl," his son replied.

"Never hiss at me," his father cried. "When I want aloes, I don't want ales, I hate such names. And cameos are cameos, not cames. Yesterday I met a man who wanted four canoes—"

"Fur canes," his son put in.

"Silence!" his father shouted. "What did you learn today in school?"

"That mist is always mist, but what is mist isn't always mist," his son recited.

At this his father rose up like a storm, put on his hat and cat, and stalked to where the door had been, and reached for where the knob once was.

"Where are yu ging?" whispered his anxious wife.

"Ut!" the boatwright cried, and ut he went.

"What did yu say t yur father that made him leave the huse?" the mother asked her son.

44

"Mist is always moist," the boy replied in whispers, "but what is moist isn't always mist."

And other odd occurrences occurred. A swain who praised his sweetheart's thrat, and said she sang like a chir of riles or a chrus of vires, was slapped. And so it went, and some lads lost their lasses, and most men lost their tempers, and all men lost their patience, and a few men lost their minds.

Then Black called Hyde one day in consultation. "Some of the people salute me as I pass," he growled. "Do you know why?"

"O-lessness is now a kind of cult in certain quar-

45

ters," Hyde observed, "a messy lessness, whose mean-inglessness nonetheless attracts the few, first one or two, then three or four, then more and more. People often have respect for what they cannot comprehend, since some men cannot always tell their crosses from their blessings, their laurels from their thorns. It shows up in the games they still can play. Charades are far more work than fun, and so are Blind Man's Buff and Hide-and-Seek, and Run, Sheep, Run. O-lessism may become the ism of the future, and men from far and wide, pilgrims on a pilgrimage, may lay their tributes on your grave."

Black showed his teeth and made a restless gesture. "Taking a single letter from the alphabet," he said, "should make life simpler."

"I don't see why. Take the F from life and you have lie. It's adding a letter to simple that makes it simpler. Taking a letter from hoarder makes it harder." With a small shrug and a little leer, Hyde turned on his heel and walked away.

Black watched him go and scowled. "He's much too smart," he said aloud, "for his own good and for mine."

There were no clocks to mark the passing hours, for Black had smashed them all. It was October now, but no one knew what day, for Black had torn from all the calendars the months with O's, October and November. Little enough was left upright, unbroken, or unravaged, and the town without its towers, and the countryside without its fountains and its pools, and the woods which had lost their oaks and hemlocks seemed deserted. The robins and the orioles had gone, and even the whippoorwill no longer sang. Then came the night the old man had predicted.

Black and Littlejack were at their table in the tavern when they heard a hue and cry, and children calling. Dogs without an O, the beagles, bassets, and the spaniels, set up a mournful howling. A wondrous light filled all the sky.

"What revelry is this?" demanded Black.

"I know not what," said Littlejack, "but I don't like it."

"I don't like it, I don't like it," squawked the parrot, and Black squcked his thrug till all he could whupple was geep.

"Geep," whuppled the parrot.

Black and Littlejack strode to where the door had been, walking on earth because the floor was gone, and stared up toward the sky. An enormous castle, lighted as by the light of many moons, stood upon a hill a mile away.

"A castle!" cried Black. He rubbed his gloves together and he gloated. "The jewels!" he cried. "The emeralds, the rubies, and the sapphires!"

"Not so fast," warned Littlejack.

"Faster!" cried Black, and he hurried through the

48

night, stumbling on the torn-up cobbles of the streets, his shining eyes upon the shining castle.

"Not so fast," warned Littlejack again. "I smell the smell of trickery and ruse."

"I smell the smell of jewels," Black exclaimed. "I smell a map."

Their crew had gathered round them now with their axes and their spades and their cudgels, yelping like a pack of hungry hounds, and they all surged toward the castle, urged on by Stragg and Strugg.

From where they stood in the shadow of a broken column, Andreus and Andrea watched them go. "This is their wildest night, and I hope it is their last," breathed Andreus.

"Keep saying hope," the old man said, appearing out of nowhere, "for we shall need it."

"There is a footnote in the book," said Andrea, "which I forgot to mention."

"How does it read?" asked Andreus.

"That if the men who seek their heart's desire

within the castle find it not before the hour of noon tomorrow, their cause is lost."

"It gives them two long hours and ten, and they must have a hundred men," said Andreus.

"I could find a map in half that time and all alone," the old man said, "if I were young."

"The map is not their heart's desire; it is the jewels," said Andrea. "And there is something in the book about a vast frustrating forest."

"How goes that part?" asked Andreus.

"It was written all in O, or nearly so, and all the O's are gone," said Andrea. "When coat is cat, and boat is bat, and goatherd looks like gathered, and booth is both, since both are bth, the reader's eye is bothered."

"And power is pwer, and zero zer, and, worst of all, a hero's her." The old man sighed as he said it.

"Anon is ann, and moan is man." Andrea smiled as she said it.

"And shoe," Andreus said, "is she."

"Ah, woe," the old man said, "is we."

Black and Littlejack and Stragg and Strugg
and all their men scattered through the
castle like a band of mad baboons, and
their shouting and their clamor shook the shields
upon the walls. "Find the jewels or the map!" cried
Black and Littlejack. "Find the jewels or the map!"
shouted Stragg and Strugg and all their men. And
they used their axes and their cudgels on every lock
and every door, breaking into cupboards, cracking

open closets, prying off the lids of boxes, smashing clocks with spades. The hours went on and the clangor rose. Everything that had an O was opened, ransacked, and pulled apart—sofas, and couches, and ottomans, things made of onyx and ormolu, ivory and ebony, gold and chalcedony, crocks and bowls, pillows and cushions and footstools, and even flagons and goblets. The men drank wine from bottles, white and red and *rosé*, and then they smashed the bottles. Boards were taken up, and marble floors, but no jewels came to light, or any map, no glow or gleam or glitter, no sight of parchment.

The moon went down; the sun began to climb the heavens. The clamor and the clangor ceased. Everything that could be broken had been broken. Glass and splinters, bits and fragments lay upon the floors, or where the floors had been. Then the wild-eyed Black raised his clenched gloves toward the sky and in that moment saw the map. It hung upon a wall, the only one left standing.

"I have not seen this wall before," cried Black.

"It was not here a moment since," cried Littlejack. "I'd lay to that."

They took the map down from the wall and spread it on a plank and bent above it, and in the end deciphered all its marks and crosses.

"The treasure lies five thousand feet from where this skull is grinning," shouted Black. "We come first to a stricken oak and count off fifty paces."

"Nor', nor'east," cried Littlejack.

"The jewels are ours," Black gloated. "We're princes!"

"Kings!" bawled Littlejack. And Stragg and Strugg and all their men echoed "Kings!" But there was no echo to their echo, for all the walls were gone. They saw before them now a dark and gloomy forest, stretching on and on, and on and farther.

"Spades!" commanded Black. "And follow me!" Then each man seized his spade and followed Black and Littlejack and Stragg and Strugg into the dark and gloomy forest.

"How goes the day?" cried Black.

"It lacks two hours of noon," said Littlejack.

"I hate the sound of noon," said Black. "I know not why."

"Perhaps because it has two O's," said Stragg.

"Perhaps because the day grows hot," said Strugg.

"And treasure should be dug up in the night," said Littlejack.

"Silence," thundered Black, "and follow me. The weather here is strange. I hate this weather."

"Why is it so hard," asked Littlejack, "to stay to-

gether?" And even as he spoke he found himself alone. He called and got no answer.

"This way," cried Black, "and all men follow me. I feel the jewels burning in my hands. I have the map and a compass. Find the stricken oak!" His voice ended in a gurgle and a croak. And then his eyes grew wide with fear, his fingers trembled, for he stood all alone, like all the others. The going underfoot was slow and oozy, for burrowing moles had devoured the roots and softened the soil.

"There are no outlets and no openings," cried Black. "It's soggy and it's boggy."

A million moths hovered above his shoulders and countless chameleons changed color on gloomy growths. Glowworms glowed around and about, and Black could not make out where he was going. Then came the butterflies. "Butterflies do not have O's," cried Black, but he was wrong. The monarchs and the morning cloaks, the clouded yellows, and all their colleagues and their fellows made up the throng. The sun went out and it seemed night again.

"What is this woeful wood?" Black whimpered,
and no one answered.

"What is this woeful wood?" croaked Littlejack,
lost and all alone in another part of the forest. The
dark was deep as midnight all around. "Whence comes
this humming and this buzzing?" wailed Littlejack.
And then he saw the source of the ominous sounds:
locusts and hornets and dragonflies, yellowjackets and
honeybees. They came in clouds and hosts and squad-
rons. "Black never thought of *little* things," mourned
Littlejack, "when he was issuing edicts." He groped
his way slowly into an outlandish grove, but there his

way was clogged by a growth of toadstools and mushrooms and monkshood and bloodroot, foxglove, wolfbane and aconite, orchids and opium poppies, and the roots of mandragora. Spanish moss drooped down and Spanish bayonets shot up. "What are these woeful worts?" muttered Littlejack, now up to his ankles and his knees in worts: bloodwort, dragonwort, goutwort, hogwort, holewort, hoodwort, lousewort, moonwort, moorwort, scorpionwort, throatwort, toothwort, and woundwort.

"What woeful wood is this?" squealed Hyde, lost and all alone in another part of the forest. Odd lights blinded him with their glow and glare and glitter: St. Elmo's fire and foxfire, will-o'-the-wisp and phosphorus, and the aurora borealis. "These are the lights of night, and not of day," moaned Hyde, "and yet I thought I saw the dawn a few hours since." He stared up at the sky, seeking the sun, and the cold O of Canopus stared down at him. The Southern Cross seemed to point its stars at him like fingers, comets and meteors flared like flaming arrows, and Virgo blazed, Capricorn, and Scorpio, the Major Dogstar and the Minor, and so many others, Hyde lost count of stars and constellations.

Then the lights went out and darkness reigned once more, and in the darkness came a show of fireworks:

rockets dropping colorful balloons, Roman candles, flowerpots, and golden showers, and silver fountains. And now there were owls and crows, loons and woodcocks, herons and flamingos, cormorants and condors, and one albatross with an arrow from a crossbow in its feathers, swooping and stooping about his head like bombers. He stumbled on, plagued by a scourge of mosquitoes, microbes, and microorganisms, through sycamore and hemlock, cottonwood and hickory, black and honey locust, oak and giant redwood, and underfoot, frogs and toads in woad hindered and hampered and harassed his going. "Incompetent, irrelevant, and immaterial," he murmured, and all the other lawyer talk that lawyers talk in triplicate. Suddenly a swoop of swans attacked him. "Objec-

tion!" Hyde implored. "Swans have no O's." Then
he recalled the cob and cos, or male and female swan.
"Confusion on creatures without an O that have an O
in their alias," shouted Hyde, and even as he spoke a
lynx was snarling at his feet. "The bobcat," whimpered Hyde. A puma showed its gleaming fangs.
"The mountain lion," quavered Hyde. "But here's
a camel! I can ride!"

"I am the dromedary," the camel said, or seemed
to say, and then it closed one eye, and opened it, and
went away.

"Imponderable, impalpable, and improbable,"
shouted Hyde. A nightingale beat its wings before
his eyes. "*Je suis le rossignol*," it sang.

"Impossible," raved Hyde, "irreverent and un-
fair."

Three bears transpired, in legal lingo, which means
they happened, took place, and occurred. "*Les ours*,
in French!" Hyde screamed. "Moreover, further-
more, and too: the cinnamon, the polar, and the
brown." He took four wobbly hops and toppled and
fell down.

All of a sudden the way grew clearer for Black in his dark part of the forest, and the sun shone bright. The earth beneath his feet seemed firmer. The threatening trees had disappeared except for one, all that was left of a stricken oak, standing in a clearing. And then he saw the long gaunt form of Littlejack, and Stragg and Strugg, and all their men, gathered about a certain spot and pointing with their spades, bitten and stung, and ruffled and rumpled, but screaming in glee and delight.

"This is the place!" cried Littlejack.

"Dig," croaked Black. And the men were about to dig with their spades, but their hands were stayed as they raised them by an ominous clamor and clangor, a snow of arrows and a sound of armor. Many figures of men loomed up, afoot or on horses, and they rode and ran among the crew, and the crew let drop their spades.

"These are but figures of fantasy," cried Black. "These men have no blood in their veins."

"Dig," bawled Littlejack, but no man dug. They stood as if rooted in the ground and gazed at the apparitions.

"Ink runs in their veins, immortal ink, the ink of song and story." It was the voice of Andreus.

"Ink can be destroyed," cried Black, "and men who are made of ink. Name me their names!"

They came so swiftly from the skies Andreus couldn't name them all, streaming out of lore and legend, streaming out of song and story, each phantom flaunting like a flag his own especial glory: Lancelot and Ivanhoe, Athos, Porthos, Cyrano, Roland, Rob Roy, Romeo; Donalbane of Birnam Wood,

60

Robinson Crusoe and Robin Hood ; the moody Doones of *Lorna Doone*, Davy Crockett and Daniel Boone ; out of near and ancient tomes, Banquo's ghost and Sherlock Holmes ; Lochinvar, Lothario, Horatius, and Horatio ; and there were other figures, too, darker, coming from the blue, Shakespeare's Shylock, Billy Bones, Quasimodo, Conrad's Jones, Ichabod and Captain Hook—names enough to fill a book.

"These wearers of the O, methinks, are indestructible," wailed Littlejack.

"Books can be burned," croaked Black.

"They have a way of rising out of ashes," said Andreus.

"I have a woeful feeling, as if the double O of doom were sticking in my throat." Black's voice, though choked, grew brighter. "The phantoms pass," he cried. "Take up your spades!" But as if this were a signal or sign, the air was filled with sudden laughter, and other figures began circling above and about the vandals like laughing Indians riding ponies, led by Mother Goose astride a broom.

"Who are these spawn of nightmare or of fever?" demanded Black.

This time it was Andrea's voice that answered him : "Little Jack Horner come out of his corner, Tommy Trout and the cat he pulled out, poor Cock Robin

and Bessy Brooks, Simple Simon and Tommy Snooks, Dr. Foster come home from Gloucester, Little Boy Blue and King Cole, too, and a certain old woman who lived in a shoe."

"These are but shadows," quavered Black. "I ripped the O from heroes and from fools!"

"But not from love," said Andrea, "or from affection, and not from memory or recollection."

"Pick up your spades!" ordered Black, laughing

so his men would laugh, but no one laughed. Then other shadows rode like thunder from the skies: the Argonauts and Myrmidons and Amazons, Adonis and Endymion, Apollo and Hyperion, and high above them, flying faster, Pollux and his brother Castor, burning like a flame in spars, lighting up the sky like stars.

Then came the great O giants: Cormoran and Blunderbore, Goliath and a hundred more, the Cyclops, hurling peaks at Noman, and even the Abominable Himalayan Snowman.

The men were prostrate now upon the ground, and all their eyes were closed against the visions from the sky.

"Dig," croaked Black, "or I shall slay you!" He drew his pistol from his belt, and Littlejack his cutlass. Fearing death far more than apparition, the men began to dig, and as they dug, a clock began to strike,

an unseen clock. The earth was suddenly hard and cold, and the blades of spades were bent and broken. "You've struck a chest," cried Black, "an ironbound chest and oaken." But what the men had struck was carbonate and carborundum, conglomerate or puddingstone, and something known as oölite or dogger. The clock continued striking. "I destroyed all clocks," cried Black.

"All clocks save one," said Andreus, "the clock that strikes in conscience." The deep tones of the clock went on until the clock had struck eleven. And on this stroke a curious phenomenon occurred. Upon the ground, and all around, appeared a score of objects, each one different from the others.

"Containers!" Black's voice was hollow. "I should have destroyed containers, and the things contained therein. A curse on Hyde and his collective nouns!"

"What is in these things I do not know, but not a single one of them contains an O." Littlejack's voice was bleak as he gazed at the odd collection: a chest, a trunk, a valise, and all sorts of cases, a barrel, a bag, and a bin, and all sorts of vases.

"A sack, a bucket, and a basket," cried Black, "a crate, an urn, and even a casket." His eyes grew dark and then they lit with a fiendish lightning. "The jewels!" he cried. "The precious stones!"

And Black and Littlejack, and Stragg and Strugg and all their men began opening the O-less containers, and in each one they found a single sheet of paper. And on each sheet a single word appeared, that gleamed and glowed and glittered. The clock struck twelve.

"It's noon," cried Black, and all the people echoed, "Noon!"

Then they heard the ringing of a distant bell, sounding near and sounding nearer, ringing clear and ringing clearer, till all the sky was filled with music as by magic.

"Freedom!" Andreus cried, naming the gleaming word the men had found, the word that glowed and glittered.

"Freedom!" Andrea echoed after him, and the sound of the greatest word turned the vandals pale and made them tremble.

"I knew the word could not be doom," the old man said, "or sorrow. I was afraid that it might be tomorrow."

And then, as by a miracle of motion, the vandals stood upon the shore, and all the
people of the island stood about them.
"Your hour has struck," said Andreus. "Here is your
ship. Begone."

"The gangway and the decks are oozy with oysters!" cried Black, "and Portuguese men-of-war, and lobsters and an octopus. And swordfish are sawing something below the waterline, urged on by a horrid school of chortling porpoises!"

Hyde was suddenly up to his ankles in phantasmagoria. "Crabs, crayfish, prawns, shrimps," he howled, "alias the decapods. Centipedes and spiders, alias the arthropods. Snails and slugs, alias mollusks and gastropods." He thought he saw crickets, too, alias orthoptera, and a score of zooming bats, alias chiroptera. He turned and ran, pursued by rodents small and big, the rat, the rabbit, and the guinea pig.

The unseen clock struck one. "The mouse is running down the clock. I see him run," said Littlejack. And all the crew saw things that weren't there as they clambered aboard the ship and set her gloomy sails, and headed slowly out to sea. And then, beyond the far horizon, the great O storms began to rage and roar, the hurricanes,* the typhoon and the monsoon, the cyclone and tornado, and there were cloudbursts and waterspouts and fog and snow, and whirlpools and maelstroms, and other odd phenomena, each with its O. The night came on and in the light of lightning

* Connie, Dorothy and Flora, Imogene and Josephine and Nora.

67

there were those on shore who saw, or thought they saw, the head of the giant Orion rising out of the sea. And there were those on shore who saw, or thought they saw, the vengeful ships of the great explorers: Columbus, De Soto, Cortez and Balboa, and all of the others since Jason and since Noah.

No word was ever heard of Black or Littlejack again, or Stragg or Strugg, or any of their men. A broken spar was washed upon the shore one day, and one black glove, but that was all. The outlawed lawyer Hyde, looking for a loophole in the law through which he might escape, was caught in one whose O's collapsed and buried him beneath its wreckage. And as he fell he heard another O, sounded by an old owl in a mossy oak, a little like an oboe obbligato.

Working with valor and love and hope, the islanders put the O back in everything that had lost it. The name of Goldilocks regained its laughter, and there were locks for keys, and shoes were no longer shes. A certain couple once more played their fond duets on mandolin and glockenspiel. Ophelia Oliver, who had vanished from the haunts of men, returned, wearing both her O's again.

Otto Ott could say his name without a stammer, and dignity returned to human speech and English grammar. Once more a man could say boo to a goose, and tell the difference between to lose and too loose. Every family had again a roof and floor, and the head of the house could say in English, as before: "Someone open (or close) the door." Towers rose up again and fountains sparkled. In the spring the robin and the oriole returned. The crows were loud in caucus, and the whippoorwill sang once again at night. The wounds that Black and Littlejack had made were healed by morning-glories, columbine, and clover, and a spreading comforter of crocuses. One April morning, Andreus and Andrea were wed.

"It could have been worse," the old man said, riding back home from the wedding. "They might have taken A. Then we would have had no marriage, or even carriage, or any walks to walk on." He wiped a tear from his eye. He was worrying about the loss of I, if I had been forbidden, when he came upon the lovers in a garden. "What would have happened," he asked them both, "without indivisibility?"

"Or, for the matter of that," said Andreus, "invincible?"

"Invincible," the old man said, "is a matter of O."

"What O?" asked Andreus and Andrea together.

"The O, lest we forget," the old man said, "in freedom."

Suddenly their thoughtful silence was changed to laughter. "Squck his thrug," they heard the parrot squawking.

"He must have missed the ship," said Andrea.

"And now he has the freedom of screech," said Andreus.

And they took the green parrot into their cottage, and in the end he was squawking, "Watch the sea!" And whenever they heard this warning and alarm, the islanders sprang to their ramparts and their towers, and scanned the sea for sinister ships with sinister sails.

Many years went by, and then one day a very old man with a long white beard stood at the base of a towering shaft of marble, surmounted, high up in the sky, with a single letter of the alphabet that glowed and gleamed and glittered in every light and weather.

"What a strange statue," a little boy cried. "A statue to a circle."

"What a strange monument," a little girl laughed. "A monument to zero."

The old man sighed and scratched his head, and thought and thought, and then he said, "It has a curious and wondrous history."

"Was it a battle? And did we win?" the children cried.

The old man shook his head and sighed, "I'm not as young as I used to be, and the years gone by are a mystery, but 'twas a famous victory."

The sun went down, and its golden glow lighted with fire the wonderful O.